THE MANUAL

The Bible

THE MANUAL
BIBLE NOTES FOR MEN

THE **Bible**

Getting to grips
with God's Word

NATHAN BLACKABY

CWR

Copyright © Nathan Blackaby 2016

Published 2017 by CWR, Waverley Abbey House, Waverley Lane, Farnham, Surrey GU9 8EP, UK. CWR is a Registered Charity – Number 294387 and a Limited Company registered in England – Registration Number 1990308.

The right of Nathan Blackaby to be identified as the author of this work has been asserted by him in accordance with the Copyright, Designs and Patents Act 1988.

For a list of National Distributors visit www.cwr.org.uk/distributors

All Scripture references are from the Holy Bible: New Living Translation, copyright © 1996, 2004, 2015 by Tyndale House Foundation. Used by permission of Tyndale House Publishers Inc., Carol Stream, Illinois 60188. All rights reserved.

Concept development, editing, design and production by CWR

Printed in the UK by Linney

ISBN: 978-1-78259-677-6

Nathan

Nathan Blackaby is the Executive Director of CVM (Christian Vision for Men), a global movement focused on introducing men to Jesus Christ. Nathan leads the team at CVM, speaking to and reaching thousands of men each year with the gospel.

Contents

Part 3: The Church and its Journey

Introduction

The Bible. Maybe you've had a flick through it before, or heard a vicar talk from it at a wedding or funeral. Or maybe you've seen one in a hotel next to the complementary shortbread but always gone down the biscuit route...

As Christians, the Bible is important because it is God's Word. It reveals His design, plan and even His character over many years. We can trust its authority and message.

The point of this book about the Bible is not to throw a tonne of information at you so that at the end you have a degree in theology and can legitimately grow a big, grey beard and become deeply intellectual. The idea here is that after you have read this book, you can pick up a Bible and get a picture of who God is and what He has to say about your life. My hope is that you will begin to lean into the Bible, trust it, explore it and mine it. The Bible will amaze you, captivate you, and when you least expect it, it will guide your life in some of the most profound ways you could ever imagine.

I used to think the Bible was out of date, much like the mullet, Vanilla Ice or the Rover Vitesse. (Some fellas have even tried to tell me that beards are the next mullets! I'm not having that, ever!) But the more you read the Bible, the more you will discover that it is relevant for not only the stuff we see and hear every day in our lives, but also about who we are and who we are meant to be.

God's Word, the Bible, has remained unchanged. It contains real-life testimonies about people's encounters with God, either personally or in a community, which at times can be very real and very messy.

The God who is revealed in the stories, events and situations of the Bible hasn't changed either. You see, the world around us and the years haven't changed the truth that you find in the Bible. The Rover Vitesse sadly became irrelevant because society, culture and commerce control what's 'in' and what's 'out'. That doesn't happen with the Bible. It's not fashionable for a season and then out again; it's not relevant then irrelevant. It's consistent. It's about real power to change lives.

Let me be clear here: the Bible is vast, and we are just skating around the edge, painting an outline to explore within. Be ready for it to challenge you, speak into your life and sometimes call you out.

Let's go.

PART 1

Building a Foundation

01 God

'In the beginning God created'
Genesis 1:1

The Bible is actually a collection of 'books' in which different situations and moments in history are recorded.

In total there are 66 books in the Bible, split into the Old Testament (the first bit), which has 39 books, and the New Testament (the second bit), which has 27 books. The first five books of the Bible are formally called the Pentateuch. This simply means 'five scrolls'. These were a conclusive history lesson; when one scroll ended, the other started.

The Old Testament talks a lot about the people of Israel, who were chosen by God to be His people at a particular time in history. They were a people who would discover who God was, why He had made them, and what a relationship with Him was all about. God had a long-term plan, and this is what unfolds and runs right through the Bible like a thread: the promise of a Saviour, the final solution to a problem the Bible calls sin.

Between the end of the Old Testament and the start of the New Testament is a period of about 400 years, during which God didn't seem to reveal His plans to humans. After that we jump into the New Testament, where the promise of a Saviour (seen in the Old Testament) is actually being fulfilled!

So, here we are at Genesis 1:1, right at the very beginning. And what's the first thing that we discover about God?

God 'created'. The Bible doesn't expand on atoms and explosions – it just says God created *everything*. First and foremost, God chooses to reveal to us that He makes, and that what He makes is amazing. It has purpose, a plan, design, form and shape that is incredible. And the good news is that this includes us too.

What does it mean to you that God created you with a purpose, a huge value and the capacity to be a man who can be used for mighty things by Him? As you explore the Bible, ask the Holy Spirit to bring it to life as you read. This is God's Word and He will speak to you through it! Get ready. Have a read of Genesis chapter 1.

01

02

Adam

'Then the LORD God called to the man, "Where are you?"' Genesis 3:9

The Bible began with a wonderful act of creativity and God's extravagance. Just look out the window, or dig under the ground and you'll see that the variety of creation is incredible. The detail and the microscopic wonder are just breathtaking. There is stuff so intricately made that you and I will probably live our whole lives not even noticing it is there.

God made Adam, and then He made Eve. How did He do it? Well, like we saw in Genesis 1, the Bible says, 'God created man'. We don't get a genome-coding diagram in the Bible, it just says that God formed man, then took a rib from the man and made woman. Genesis was never meant to be a science textbook. It focuses on the *why*s of creation, not the *how*s. And the reason is revealed to be a relationship; all of creation was made to enjoy the creator. The Bible describes Adam and Eve as walking in the presence of God with no barrier and no limitation.

But then something happened. A problem came into the world, and the Bible calls that problem 'sin'. In the New Testament, in a book called James, you read this: 'Temptation comes from our own desires, which entice us and drag us away. These desires give birth to sinful actions. And when sin is allowed to grow, it gives birth to death' (James 1:14-15).

Sin found its way into the centre of God's creation. Adam and Eve, the founding couple of all of humanity, turned their hearts from God and sin moved in. A break in the perfect relationship between humanity and God happened at that moment; huge and dividing. Adam blames Eve, Eve blames the devil, but the damage is done and they are now hiding from God instead of walking with Him.

The result of sin is death, and once that infected the human race it was like corrupted code entering our DNA. Everyone born from that day on came under that curse of sin. It's fair to say that a rescue mission was most definitely needed!

Have you ever thought about sin in your life? What has that looked like or felt like? Speak to God today about where you are in your relationship with Him. Just be honest.

03

Noah

'Noah was a righteous man, the only blameless person living on earth at the time, and he walked in close fellowship with God.' **Genesis 6:9**

The Bible is full of true stories of men and women who have stood and trusted God, sometimes even at great personal cost. Noah comes onto the scene during a time when sin has ravaged humanity's love for God.

This is probably one of the most famous stories found in the Bible. You might remember it from school or Sunday school talks about the rainbow, but the reality of it is shocking.

Noah was the *only one* who hadn't turned his heart and life away from God. The Bible tells us that God saw the wickedness in the hearts of His creation and regretted making them, and initiated a plan to wipe out humanity. But Noah found God's grace.

You might remember the story... a great big boat, lots of animals, loads of rain, and Noah and his family survived. It's well worth a read. But the point I want to highlight in this is God's grace. Something that you will find time and time again as you explore the Bible is that people full of flaws and mess and sin discover God's grace when they really turn back to Him.

The image many people have of God is a white-bearded, cuddly old man. The picture of God in the Bible smacks that right out of the park as we are introduced to a God who invites us to call Him 'Dad', but we also see God revealed as the judge of all. Darkness has nowhere to hide from Him. He spoke words and creation was formed. God is mighty, and His authority covers the whole earth, all that is on it, in it and all that will ever be.

Yet combined with this image of God, the Bible leaves no doubt about God's grace. He pours it out over people all the time when they just don't deserve it. When they turn back to Him He lavishes grace on them. This thread of God's grace amongst His holiness is central to the Bible, and you will see it all the way through.

Have you shown grace to anyone else before? Why did you do it? Spend a moment thinking about why God might be showing you grace in your life.

03

04

Abraham

'All the families on earth will be blessed through you.' **Genesis 12:3**

If you want to discover what faith and trust in God can really look like, then Abraham is the man to watch. His life was marked with promises and carved out of patience, as He waited for God to do what He had promised.

God had promised Abraham and Sarah a child - an angel visited them and told them it was going to happen - but after 20 years, they were still waiting. (Eventually, God did come through for them.)

The stories about Abraham's life are amazing, but he wasn't a perfect man. If he couldn't see how God was going to resolve an issue, he got on with sorting it out himself. This happened a few times and even ended up with Abraham having a child (called Ishmael) with his servant instead of his wife. It didn't go very well, but again God showed grace to Abraham.

Central to Abraham's story is his role as a father, as this was a huge part of who he was and what God had called him to be. Remember God's rescue mission? Here are the foundations of that very mission, built into the lives of people throughout the Bible.

The Bible talks about 'covenants'. God makes lots of covenants, which are unbreakable promises. The Bible also includes family trees, and we can see how these covenants and promises travel through them, down the generations. God was building a group of people who would last the ages. It started here with Abraham and continued all the way along his family right up to the time of Jesus, who was part of this same family!

Abraham became a 'father of nations' – in other words, he had a huge family that stretched down through generations and across vast areas of land. His people had been selected to play a key role in the rescue mission of God. This nation features a lot in the Old Testament; their highs and lows, their sinfulness and wickedness, then their returning to God and seeing His grace.

Have you experienced times when you don't understand or see what God is doing? What helps you to trust Him in times like that?

05

Isaac

'It was by faith that even Sarah was able to have a child, though she was barren and was too old. She believed that God would keep his promise.' **Hebrews 11:11**

Isaac stands out firstly for having the oldest dad ever. Abraham hit the big 100 when Isaac was born!

Isaac was the son God had promised to Abraham and Sarah. Remember the Israelites, the group of people who God was going to be revealed through? Well, that line was going to continue with Isaac.

Have a quick read of Genesis 22 – it's a pretty mad story. Abraham is told to take Isaac to the mountain and offer him as a burnt offering. Hang on, Isaac was Abraham's only son... What about the promise of generations of family? Something has surely gone wrong here!

Isaac follows his father up the mountain and asks where the lamb is for the fire. Abraham replies, 'God will provide, son.' Hmm... I would have been asking more questions if I were Isaac.

The Bible tells us that Abraham tied Isaac up and laid him on the altar. The reason I think

Abraham and Isaac both trusted God was that, as some commentators suggest, at this point Abraham was about 120 years old and Isaac was about 20. I like to see this as Isaac actually trusting too. He could have fought, run, wrestled his old dad to the ground, but we see none of that; just surrender.

God steps in at the final moment. If you skipped reading Genesis 22, you will have to go and read it now! We start to see God looking for faith and trust in the lives of Abraham and Isaac, even in the most wild of situations. Isaac trusts God, goes on to get married and has a couple of sons, Esau and Jacob. The promise of the massive family tree keeps going with Isaac, so let's follow it...

In many ways Isaac was a normal bloke; he had a massive experience in his life that shaped him going forward. Have there been times in your life that have been groundbreaking, times that have caused you to trust in God, even when perhaps you didn't want to believe He was there?

06

Esau and Jacob

'Esau hated Jacob because their father had given Jacob the blessing. And Esau began to scheme: "I will soon be mourning my father's death. Then I will kill my brother, Jacob."' **Genesis 27:41**

Esau was born first, and then Jacob. The birth was a little bit odd because as Esau was born Jacob was hanging on to his heel on the way out. (Rebecca knew about this because she could literally feel these two wrestling in her womb; two nations, the older would serve the younger!)

By this time Isaac was old and in his last days, and he needed to bless his first-born son Esau. This was a huge part of the culture called the 'birthright'. This birthright was linked to land, possessions, animals and so on. Esau had already spoken with Jacob about handing over his birthright, but he didn't realise what was about to happen.

Esau was hungry and Jacob offered him some food but only if he sold or gave him his birthright, which Esau agreed to do. Jacob must have thought it wouldn't happen – it was as though he was just trying his luck.

Jacob stitches Esau up, big time. Read about this in Genesis 25:29–33 and chapter 27.

Remember Isaac, old and blind, waiting to bless his son Esau with the birthright? Well, Jacob pretends to be Esau, puts animal skin on his arms because his brother was a hairy fella, and deceives dear old Isaac. Jacob gets the birthright blessing and all its goodies. Esau is, how could we put it... slightly *miffed* about it all.

We come to Genesis 32. Jacob is on the run with all his animals and family. He gets word that Esau is on his way, which can only mean one thing: a really bad end for Jacob as his deceived brother finally gets his vengeance on them all. Jacob goes into a complete panic, sending his family left and right to escape, then sits in the middle just waiting for Esau.

That night he wrestles with God and refuses to let go until God blesses him! So he gets his blessing and a name change, no longer the 'deceiver', but now called 'Israel'!

Jacob wasn't the perfect bloke, but God still did amazing things in his life. Don't dwell on the mess you might have made or the times you've slipped up, but remember that God can and does work in people who others would write off.

---

07 Joseph

'The LORD was with Joseph, so he succeeded in everything he did'
Genesis 39:2

Jacob had a big family. There were four women in his life, who gave him twelve sons, who then went on to form the twelve tribes (or families) of Israel... and now Abraham's promise of a huge family is gathering momentum. A significant thing here is that Jesus followed in this family line. Rebecca gave birth to Gad, Asher, Joseph and Benjamin, and Jesus' human birth line goes from Adam and weaves its way along the line through Abraham, Isaac, Jacob and now Joseph.

You might remember the story of Joseph: Jacob had given him a 'Technicolor' coat because he loved Joseph the most. Well, the coat and some dreams Joseph had meant that his brothers didn't really like him very much. One dream showed 11 stars bowing down before Joseph, and it was probably not such a great idea to share that with his 11 brothers.

The 11 brothers were seriously fed up with their 17-year-old brother and after a little bit of plotting and scheming they dumped him in a ditch, sold him to slave traders, and gave his fancy coat the *what for* so it looked like a wild animal had sorted him out. Job done... or was it? You can read this in Genesis 37:12–36.

Joseph's story is utterly covered in honesty: he was a seriously honest fella and even when the heat was on, he kept his integrity. After he was sold by slave traders into Egypt, he worked for a wealthy man whose wife made the moves on him, but he shunned her. He was unwilling to break his master's trust. Honest move, Joseph, but it ended him up in prison!

The years went by and Joseph had lost his family, job, reputation and freedom, all for being a man of integrity. But God started a rescue plan and Joseph's rise to power was incredible, one that meant his 11 brothers did bow down to him! Take some time to read the story of Joseph because not only is it incredible, it also tells how the people of Israel ended up being in Egypt as slaves. It was Joseph's family who moved there, but they weren't slaves then!

Joseph was betrayed, rejected and despised for trying to make the right decisions, but God didn't forget him. God had a plan for Joseph's life, and obedience was central to it. Be encouraged to keep doing the right thing!

08

Israel

"'I am God, the God of your father,' the voice said. "Do not be afraid to go down to Egypt, for there I will make your family into a great nation.'" **Genesis 46:3**

A lot is about to happen now. Hopefully you have managed to read those few chapters in Genesis, but if not, let's quickly bring ourselves up to speed by briefly fast-forwarding through a few hundred years.

Joseph had found favour with the Pharaoh of Egypt but a famine was going on and the Bible tells us this: 'Then Pharaoh said to Joseph, "Now that your father and brothers have joined you here, choose any place in the entire land of Egypt for them to live. Give them the best land of Egypt. Let them live in the region of Goshen. And if any of them have special skills, put them in charge of my livestock, too"' (Genesis 47:5-6).

So Israel (Jacob and his family, Joseph and his brothers and their wives, children and animals) all moved into the land and a few hundred years passed. (There is debate about the actual number of years, but it is thought to have been between 215 and 430 years.) But when the old

Pharaoh died and the new king took control, he didn't know Joseph - and as he saw how the Israelites (Abraham's promised family) made up a good chunk of the population, he didn't like it one bit (check it out in Exodus 1:8-11).

But even under slavery and oppression, the family of Israel kept on growing. So the king decided to sort this out and commanded that any Jewish sons to be born should be thrown into the river.

At this point in the story of the Old Testament then, the Hebrew people (or 'the children of Israel') are living in Egypt - about two million of them! (Only about 70 people moved there when Joseph was in charge!) Life is very hard and they are slaves; lost, hopeless, and in need of a serious rescue mission...

Throughout the whole of human history, God has always had a plan. And He is incredibly patient! Sometimes in our own lives, God will be laying some foundations and building stuff slowly, almost off our radar, but He is still at work. Maybe pause today just to look at your life and see where God has been building!

09

Moses

"'Now go, for I am sending you to Pharaoh. You must lead my people Israel out of Egypt." But Moses protested to God, "Who am I to appear before Pharaoh? Who am I to lead the people of Israel out of Egypt?"' Exodus 3:10-11

There's so much we can learn about Moses – how he was born a slave and raised a prince, only to become a murderer and a fugitive, and later a husband, father, spokesman and the man God chose to lead the Israelites out of slavery. Moses gets a good few mentions in the Bible – he was kind of a big deal!

You might have heard about the Ten Commandments, for example, which were given to Moses. Or you might remember the plagues in Egypt and an incredible escape through the parted sea! All of this stuff is found in the second book of the Bible, called Exodus, which means 'going out' or 'exit'.

It is really worth taking some time to read about the life of Moses, as he was born a Hebrew at a time when all the Hebrew sons were being thrown in the river by the king of Egypt. One of the king's daughters found Moses in a basket on the river and raised him as a prince of the Egyptian kingdom. Not too shabby!

But for now, just have a look at how Moses met God at the burning bush, something that, like many of his other experiences, changed the course of his life forever.

Moses felt inadequate; not at all up to the task. He lacked confidence and didn't feel qualified to be part of God's amazing rescue mission to bring the Jewish people out of slavery and into a land of their own. He was a murderer and fugitive, after all. And really not the best public speaker...

But even though he didn't think he was the right man for the job, he got on with it. He trusted God and gave it everything, and God used his obedience to lead the Hebrew people in some unprecedented, mass-scale, hard-core emancipation.

Moses had a glimpse of God and it literally transformed his life! What about you – have you ever wanted to catch a glimpse of God? Why not ask Him to meet with you now?

10

Mountains and commandments

'Moses remained there on the mountain with the LORD forty days and forty nights. In all that time he ate no bread and drank no water. And the LORD wrote the terms of the covenant–the Ten Commandments–on the stone tablets.' **Exodus 34:28**

Vast sections of the Old Testament in the Bible are records of measurement, instructions and family trees. While this is important for the historical accuracy of the Bible, if we're being honest, it can make for a difficult read. But these instructions and family trees actually show us so much of God's grace, mercy and desire to love His creation just as much as the bits about burning bushes and parting oceans!

Moses leads the children of Israel out of Egypt in the most incredible way. God guides them out into the wilderness and brings this nation into a new identity. The Ten Commandments are not just a set of rules, but a brand new manifesto for a nation who are called to worship God.

The customs and traditions, the rules for making an altar for the sacrifice of animals, were all given by God to help the people know how to worship Him and live in relationship with Him.

From decades of wandering the desert, the Jewish people learned the hard way that trusting and obeying God was the main ingredient in this new relationship. They wanted to be His people, to obey and serve God, but time after time they looked away from God and disobeyed Him, and it cost them.

The journey of Israel through the wilderness is huge in the Bible, and it is easy to get lost in the details when reading about it, but there is a common theme. God keeps forgiving; God keeps on picking them back up. Yes, there are consequences to their disobedience, but God continually shows them grace and mercy. And that's how He still operates today.

Have a read through the following major sections in the life of Israel:
- **The Red Sea crossing: Exodus 14**
- **The Ten Commandments: Exodus 19-20**
- **The golden calf: Exodus 32**
- **The Ten Commandments, again: Exodus 34**
- **Building the Ark of the Covenant (you know, the thing in *Raiders of the Lost Ark*!): Exodus 37:1-9**

PART 2

The Time is Now!

11
The Psalms

'I wait quietly before God, for my victory comes from him. He alone is my rock and my salvation, my fortress where I will never be shaken.' **Psalm 62:1-2**

The Psalms are essentially a collection of songs and poems that cover a varied subject matter (but the punchline is usually 'God is good'). They have a posh name too – the 'Psalter', which means 'the book of praises'.

There are 150 psalms, at least 73 of which were written by King David, and more than seven other people contributed. The collection is made up of sub-categories, but there are two main themes running through them all. The first is that God is great and does great things, and the second revolves around the individual and corporate lives of the Jewish people. These can be divided like this:

- Psalms of thanks and praise
- Psalms of lament (times when it feels like the wheels have fallen off)
- Enthronement psalms for new kings
- Royal psalms
- Wisdom psalms

Almost every psalm starts with some sort of promise, affirmation or declaration that God is good and mighty. They then move on to make a case against or in response to something that has happened, followed by a cry to God for help and a reaffirmation that even though this is a difficult situation, God is good and will help. Some psalms are written from what feels like a deep pit of despair, and others are written from the mountaintops, when all things are going as well as they can.

Let me leave you today with Psalm 51. I have used this to pray each day for over a month and I started to memorise it, which is incredible for me! Psalm 51 is from King David, when he had slept with another man's wife, then arranged for her husband to go to the front line, where he knew he would be killed. It was a messy, messy situation, but God still worked in David's life and made him into an incredible man after God's own heart!

You can discover the psalms and how you can use them as prayers in even more detail in *The Manual: Prayer.*

Try reading Psalm 51 (or another of your choice) as a prayer, or find your own words to be honest and real before God. Don't worry – He can handle it!

12

Prophecies and the Minor Prophets

'the LORD has told you what is good, and this is what he requires of you: to do what is right, to love mercy, and to walk humbly with your God.'
Micah 6:8

Prophecies in the Bible are a way in which God communicated (and still communicates today) with His people. Prophets spoke messages from God to the people. The messages varied greatly in each situation, time, purpose, and method in which they were delivered, but when they came through, it was clear that God had spoken directly into that moment.

These prophets – and the messages they were given – covered a period of time of about 400 years, so kings, people and nations grew and changed. The Jewish people were ultimately conquered and divided or exiled, both the northern and southern kingdoms. The prophets spoke during this time about what was to come and what would happen afterwards.

There are two main categories for the prophets: Minor Prophets and Major Prophets. The Minor Prophets were not all adolescents or lacking depth in their messages – they are simply called 'minor' due to their volume of prophecy. This is in comparison with the Major Prophets, who covered vast periods of time with many words for the nation. Minor or major, the words they brought packed a punch!

What is interesting about these prophets is often how they were called in the first place, and how they had to deliver the messages. For example, there was a simple fig-farming fella called Amos, and then there was Hosea, who married a promiscuous woman to show the people how they had become in the eyes of God!

These prophets foretold events that only God could have revealed to them. Their messages could be for entire nations, smaller communities or individuals, but they always involved bringing God's people back into a right relationship with Him.

God knows the start and the finish. So much of life is uncertain, but God knows you and me in the most infinite way. All is unravelled before Him and nothing is hidden. That's awesome!

13

Prophecies and the Major Prophets

'For a child is born to us, a son is given to us. The government will rest on his shoulders. And he will be called: Wonderful Counselor, Mighty God, Everlasting Father, Prince of Peace.' **Isaiah 9:6**

The major prophets in the Bible were: Isaiah, Jeremiah, Ezekiel and Daniel.

Isaiah spoke a lot of prophecy during his time. He was around during the divide of the kingdoms of Israel and Judah, and his message was clear and sharp as he challenged the behaviour of the nations. He saw them move away from being God's people and turn to follow empty rituals and religion instead. Isaiah even predicted that the Babylonians (one of the nation's neighbours) would turn up and plunder them, destroy Judah and take them off as prisoners. You guessed it... that actually happened.

So at this point it's important to get another wider snapshot of what was going on at that time. Isaiah had been delivering prophecy before the exile of both Israel and Judah, and then it happened:

they were divided and conquered and taken off to exile. After this, Daniel and Ezekiel had a lot of major prophecies during the exile of the kingdoms, then Haggai, Zechariah and Malachi were speaking during a post-exile time. Are you still with me?

The point in sharing this stuff was that the people of Israel were scattered and lost because they had turned away from God. They refused time and time again to be the people they had promised to be way back when they had left Egypt under the leadership of Moses. So they needed help, and they knew that one day God would save them and bring them back as one people – God's people. Isaiah prophesied a lot about this and about the Messiah (Saviour). Even though Isaiah spoke this stuff hundreds of years before Jesus, he was right!

In Isaiah 7:14 we are told that the Messiah would be born of a virgin, and in Matthew 1:22-23 and Luke 1:31-35, we see that's what happened. Bible commentators have found hundreds of similar prophecies made in the Old Testament and fulfilled in the New Testament.

Has anyone prophesied over you? What did they say? It's helpful to keep stuff like that written down so you can keep track of what God's doing in your life!

---

14 Jesus

'I am the way, the truth, and the life.'
John 14:6

Over 400 years after the last Old Testament prophet, the curtain goes up on the New Testament as Jesus is about to take centre stage. John the Baptist (a sort-of cousin of Jesus) began to announce the arrival of the Messiah. He called people to repent, turn away from their sinful lives, and get ready for Jesus.

The Jewish people were now part of the Roman Empire, which controlled things in the region by using King Herod as a puppet ruler. The Jews found themselves in a new culture as generations were born into a Jewish tradition with Roman rules. So they wanted liberation, freedom and the land they had been promised; they wanted a distinct identity again, and this Messiah was supposed to bring that about and beat the Roman powers.

Jesus arrived... but He didn't ride in on a horse, wielding weapons of mass destruction and commanding an undefeatable army like the Jewish people expected. Instead, He turned everything on its head, challenging every paradigm society had.

Jesus fulfilled the prophecies about Him, born of a virgin to a specific family line, at a specific time and place. At 30 years old He taught people, performed miracles, healed people, drove out demons, freed people and talked about sin and new life. Jesus pointed to His Father (not Joseph, who raised Him, but God) and He spoke as God's Son. He called people to follow Him, to live by His teaching and to accept Him as their friend and Lord. Jesus spoke about His death and burial, and about how this wouldn't be the end. He spoke about a rescue mission, where the entire human race, both then and every generation to follow, would be rescued from death and sin and find eternal life!

Lots of people accept Jesus as a 'wise teacher', a 'nice man' or even a 'prophet', but Jesus didn't call Himself that at all. He was so much more than that! His message was as God's Son, here to save us from sin and death, a free gift of life and hope, peace and forgiveness, no matter who we are.

Jesus lived, breathed our air and did what the Bible said He did. Take a moment to consider the real person of Jesus.

---

15 Disciples

'Jesus called out to them, "Come, follow me, and I will show you how to fish for people!"' **Matthew 4:19**

Jesus didn't visit the religious hotspots of the day to recruit the brightest and most promising apprentices He could. He went for the rejects – the fellas who had sat on the sidelines, never getting picked. The fishermen and tax collectors, the fringe guys, not the elite of the day. Selecting only these guys, Jesus assembled a dream team of assorted misfits. And they would change the world forever.

When the disciples realised who Jesus was, they took Him at His word. They watched Jesus, ate with Him and shadowed Him from the start to the end of the day. Jesus spoke truth to them, empowered them, and they discovered they could trust Him no matter what.

Peter was one of these disciples. He was a fisherman, and yet Jesus taught *him* how to fish! Peter realised he was sitting next to someone special. He even asked Jesus to leave him because he knew he wasn't worthy of His company. But instead, Jesus called Peter to follow Him, and be part of the biggest movement in history.

Peter got it wrong a lot; at one point he even stooped to the level of denying he knew Jesus. But even then, Jesus didn't kick him off the team, but restored him to go again! Peter was able to see thousands of people discover real life through Jesus.

But it wasn't always sunshine and roses for the disciples. They gave up control of their lives and careers and went all in. Many of them gave their lives, being killed for their refusal to deny Jesus as the Son of God. Once they had been that close to Jesus, they could never be the same again; they were new men – free men – and nothing would ever take that away.

The disciples weren't straight-A students. Jesus had to correct them, stop them from trying to compete with each other, and at times some serious ego realignment was needed. But these 12 ordinary chaps were given the amazing privilege of walking with Jesus, learning from Him and sharing His world-changing message.

Flip to Matthew 6:9-13 and have a read of the Lord's Prayer. Read the bits just before and after it as well! This is how Jesus taught His disciples to pray. How could you make it a habit of your own?

16

Matthew

'Later, as Jesus left the town, he saw a tax collector named Levi sitting at his tax collector's booth. "Follow me and be my disciple," Jesus said to him. So Levi got up, left everything, and followed him.' **Luke 5:27-28**

There are four Gospels, each named after their respective author: Matthew, Mark, Luke and John. All four were written between AD 65 and AD 95, soon after Jesus' life, death and resurrection. The first three Gospels – Matthew, Mark and Luke – are described as 'synoptic' Gospels because they have common styles, themes and ways of telling the good news, whereas John's Gospel is in a slightly different style. The four writers wrote their accounts of Jesus' life with different target audiences in mind, but taken together, the four Gospels present a testimony of Jesus.

Matthew wrote mainly to a Jewish audience – both to those who already believed in Jesus, and to those who didn't yet believe. Matthew's account highlights that Jesus is the long-awaited Messiah that the Jewish people were waiting for, by including prophetic messages from the

Old Testament to show that they were fulfilled in the life of Jesus. Matthew also gives us Jesus' genealogy at the start of the Gospel, again showing the Jewish readers the authenticity of Jesus and His family line going through King David, and back even to Abraham.

Matthew was formerly named Levi, a tax collector (widely disliked and far from being one of the religious elite). Tax collectors in Jesus' day were notorious for being corrupt, over-taxing people to make themselves rich. Matthew was utterly transformed when he met Jesus, and He gave his life to serving Him. This Gospel is an eyewitness account!

Have a read of Levi/Matthew's story in Luke 5:27-32. Don't forget these are not religious fellas – Matthew was a crook but found forgiveness when he met Jesus. Be encouraged – you don't have to get your life sorted before Jesus accepts you!

16

17 Mark

'And you must love the LORD your God with all your heart, all your soul, all your mind, and all your strength.' **Mark 12:30**

Mark's Gospel was written for a different audience to Matthew's. Mark himself was not an eyewitness to the life of Jesus, but he was a close travelling companion to Peter. Peter was a disciple and witness of Jesus, so Mark was like his wingman as they travelled around together telling people about Jesus. Mark was a Jewish Christian, in that he had accepted Jesus as the Messiah, and his family home was where the Early Church used to meet.

Mark's Gospel is mainly written to Roman Christians, and often the Bible refers to these Christ followers as 'gentiles'. 'Gentile' is a term that essentially describes those who are not Jewish. (When we look at Paul's life we will explore this a little bit more and how the good news of Jesus first went to the Jewish people, then to the Gentiles.)

Mark's Gospel contains some themes that are different to those in the other Gospels, even though many of the events described are the same. In his account, Mark is able to capture not only the fact that Jesus is God's Son, but also presents to us the humanity of Jesus. Emotions, abilities and limitations all help us to relate to Jesus as a human being. Mark doesn't list family trees or loads of prophecies, but instead looks at the works of Jesus in more detail and shows Him as a selfless servant.

In Mark 14:32–42 you can read about Jesus praying in the garden of Gethsemane just moments before His betrayal and arrest. Mark chronicles the emotional state of Jesus as He prays, knowing full well what is about to happen: a beating, flogging and hours of extreme agony as He suffers through the torture of crucifixion. Mark captures the humanity of Jesus in this powerful moment. This is an incredible picture of Jesus – not as a baby in a manger, or a smirking face with a halo, but a man – God's Son in anguish and pain, preparing Himself for the worst suffering imaginable.

Life can throw us some real curveballs at times, and we can feel like God doesn't understand, and nor does anyone else. What Mark helps us see here is that Jesus fully understands. Maybe just spend a moment now in stillness to think about this, and the chaos you might be facing.

18

Luke

'As the time drew near for him to ascend to heaven, Jesus resolutely set out for Jerusalem.' **Luke 9:51**

Luke's Gospel account is a bit different. Luke was an educated Greek and he knew his stuff. He used the most sophisticated Greek word forms with impeccable detail. Luke was a detailed historian and the little things mattered to him in the way he wrote his account. He had done his research, and indicates that he has drawn this stuff from eyewitness accounts and from his time working with Paul, so his accuracy is reliable.

Not an awful lot is known about Luke other than that he was a Gentile, he most likely had a medical background (referred to as a physician or doctor), and he was a travelling companion of Paul. It is thought that Paul was in prison in Rome when Luke was writing his Gospel account.

Before we look at the themes running through Luke's Gospel, it is worth mentioning that Luke also wrote a follow-up to this, called Acts. Not only was Luke among just a handful of Gentile authors to have written in the Bible, but the book of Acts is an amazing account of the Early Church.

Acts – or 'Acts of the Apostles' as it can be called – is about the stuff the Early Church (the first Christians) did after Jesus' resurrection and ascension. The Church did some amazing things back then, but also faced some extraordinarily tough times.

The themes in Luke's Gospel focus on showing Jesus as the 'Son of Man', a common term in Luke's record of the life, death and resurrection of Jesus. Luke also goes into detail about how Jesus empowered, loved and showed compassion to an unusual set of people – women, children, sinners, outcasts, and people sitting way off the social radar of the time.

The verse I included at the start of this section is important as it is like Luke's 'lift off' button. The first nine chapters build up to Luke shifting gear and taking the reader on a ten-chapter journey as Jesus heads to the cross. Luke shows Jesus focused and purposeful about the cross – the reason for the mission.

Read a few chapters of Luke in your Bible. Some translations say that Jesus 'set His face like flint'. Here's the thing: Jesus went through it all to rescue us. It cost Him everything on that cross, but He won!

---

19 John

'But these are written so that you may continue to believe that Jesus is the Messiah, the Son of God, and that by believing in him you will have life by the power of his name.'
John 20:31

John's Gospel is the last one for us to look at, and the verse above is renowned for being John's purpose for writing his account: so that people would trust and believe that Jesus is the Son of God.

John's book is more spiritual than the others. It focuses more on the spiritual impact and narrative of the life of Jesus. John and his brother James were friends and followers of Jesus, and Jesus gave them the title 'Sons of Thunder' due to their nature and character (temper, temper), but John ended up with a legacy all about love. He was obsessed with love!

John also worked with Peter after Jesus had returned to heaven, and even became a huge influence in the church in Jerusalem. John would probably have known of the other Gospels and contributed his own angle with eyewitness accounts combined with a spiritual flavour.

John also wrote some letters (1, 2 and 3 John) and the book of Revelation, the final book in the Bible.

John includes some interesting themes in his Gospel account. Particularly important to him were signs that point to Jesus' identity as the Son of God. These signs are there to help people believe, trust and ultimately discover life. These are central to his writing, but there are a few sub-themes too. He talked about light, dark, life, death, above, below, love, hate... John often spoke in this kind of dualistic way to get his point across powerfully. As you read John, try to have an awareness of some of the imagery that springs to mind.

John also recorded some 'I am' sayings of Jesus, which punch out a clear message with no doubt or uncertainty about who it is that John wants you to see in his account – the vine, the good shepherd... Check them out!

Take some time to find some of these 'I am' sayings in your Bible. Check out John 6:35; 8:12; 10:7,9; 10:11,14; 11:25; 14:6; 15:1,5.

20

The Holy Spirit

'Suddenly, there was a sound from heaven like the roaring of a mighty windstorm, and it filled the house where they were sitting. Then, what looked like flames or tongues of fire appeared and settled on each of them. And everyone present was filled with the Holy Spirit and began speaking in other languages, as the Holy Spirit gave them this ability.' **Acts 2:2-4**

Pentecost was the moment when God's Holy Spirit rocked up. The Holy Spirit is the third part of the Trinity – God – and by Him we are born again as Christians and empowered to do the work He has for us to do! If you've decided to follow Jesus, that means you have the Holy Spirit living inside you – yes, you – now!

One of the main things Jesus accomplished on the cross and in His resurrection, besides paying the penalty for sin, was to open up the offer of freedom to everyone, not just the Jews. So at Pentecost, the Holy Spirit arrived as Jesus had promised. And He knew how to make an entrance!

Holy Spirit stuff isn't always all about speaking in tongues, prophesying and healing (although He certainly is in the business of all those things!). The Holy Spirit does all sorts. Let's look at what Jesus said about the Holy Spirit before He returned to heaven: 'But when the Father sends the Advocate as my representative—that is, the Holy Spirit—he will teach you everything and will remind you of everything I have told you' (John 14:26).

Just in this verse alone, Jesus presents the Holy Spirit as a friend; advocate; counsellor; teacher; someone who would dwell with us and in us, and will empower us when we believe.

This might sound weird, but the Holy Spirit is like the DNA of the Church. The Church isn't defined by buildings, but by people - that is where the Holy Spirit dwells and works.

Maybe you have already decided to follow Jesus; maybe you haven't, and you're drilling into this stuff for more info. You might want to pray today - just a simple prayer that asks the Holy Spirit to help you explore this stuff and for Him to make Himself real in your life.

PART 3

The Church and its Journey

21

Stephen

'A great wave of persecution began that day, sweeping over the church in Jerusalem; and all the believers except the apostles were scattered through the regions of Judea and Samaria.' **Acts 8:1**

This may seem like a bit of a curveball to throw in, but what the Bible records here is actually a significant turning point for the Early Church and the next section of books that we see in the Bible.

The Church huddled together after Jesus ascended back to heaven. Believers were meeting up, growing in their faith and doing some really exciting stuff, but then calamity struck.

Stephen was a solid guy. The Bible says he was full of the Holy Spirit and totally genuine. But what he spoke about – Jesus – upset people. Not long before that, the Pharisees had wanted Jesus killed, so the last thing they wanted was Stephen telling people that Jesus wasn't dead and was in fact God's Son! But Stephen would not be silenced, so they dragged him outside so they could stone him to death. Stephen didn't fight or try to defend himself; he even asked God to forgive his executioners. This moment was the start of lots of persecution of the Church, which is still happening 2,000 years later.

The Roman emperor at that time, Nero, was a brutal ruler and had many Christians killed in horrific ways. The result was that the Church scattered, only not to hide, but to share the good news even wider! The Church had been building strength and momentum, and Stephen's death triggered a movement outward for the Church... It started to go global.

The reason this is important is that the next sections we'll explore record the journeys, the letters and the teaching that went out to all these new churches and individuals. Little by little, one life at a time, the truth of Jesus was turning from whispers to shouts! New life had been made available; the Messiah had come and defeated death. Now that was good news – it still is today!

Have a read of Acts 8, and see how the word began to spread after Stephen's death. How amazing that even something as terrible as this was used by God as an incredible, positive force for the Early Church! Redemptive or what?

22

Paul

'My old self has been crucified with Christ. It is no longer I who live, but Christ lives in me. So I live in this earthly body by trusting in the Son of God, who loved me and gave himself for me.' **Galatians 2:20**

The apostle Paul ('apostle' essentially means 'one who is sent out') now takes a major role in the writings of the New Testament.

Paul was a missionary pioneer. He travelled on three key journeys across the Mediterranean landscape and effectively carried the good news of Jesus throughout the Roman Empire. Paul was beaten up, arrested, stoned, chased out of towns and communities, shipwrecked, imprisoned and likely beheaded in Rome (although the Bible doesn't confirm this). But during Paul's lifetime he was able to encourage and inspire generations of people as he travelled, tirelessly sharing the truth about Jesus.

Yet perhaps one of the most amazing things about Paul is the fact that at the time of Stephen's death, Paul was standing there cheering on the men throwing the rocks at Stephen.

Yep – Paul was once known as Saul, and he wasn't a nice guy. He'd been raised as a Roman citizen but was from the tribe of Benjamin, one of the Israelite families, so his family line went back to Abraham. He was also raised as a Pharisee, who were the strictest Jewish sect of the time, and rigorously kept the laws from Moses' encounter with God hundreds of years before.

Saul was persecuting the Christians. He absolutely hated them and was on his way to Damascus to arrest some more when he had a revelation – a vision of Jesus. Saul's life was so dramatically transformed that he went from hater to key evangelist and turned the world upside down.

When Paul became a follower of Jesus it was a game-changer. A man who had actively persecuted and exterminated Christians became one of the most effective evangelists in history. And he wrote a good chunk of the New Testament, too! Read about his life for yourself in Acts 9:1-20.

Is there anyone you've ever considered to be too bad for God? Why not pray that God would break into their life and use them for His purposes?

23

The letters to churches and people

'This letter is from Paul, chosen by the will of God to be an apostle of Christ Jesus, and from our brother Timothy.' **Colossians 1:1**

So, we have a picture of the scene: the Church was scattered, the disciples travelled and shared Jesus everywhere they went. Saul had been persecuting the Church, but his life changed dramatically after an encounter with Jesus, and he became known as Paul.

Paul went on three main missionary journeys, sharing the truth about Jesus with incredible signs and wonders as he went. He himself was arrested, and during these times in prison or under house arrest (which allowed a bit more freedom), Paul was able to start writing letters to encourage the churches he had established, as well as to individuals within those churches and younger leaders. We find some of these letters in the New Testament.

Often these letters will start with a greeting from Paul and some of his own personal thanks or prayers for the people he is writing to. Then he sets about doing a few key things. He reminds the churches of what he has taught them or what they have heard concerning the truth about Jesus. He offers practical advice and helps deal with difficult situations (or people) within the church. Paul also teaches about what the Christian life should look like, how to conduct the church format, and how to ensure that what is being taught is true and right.

Some of Paul's letters might feel like a teacher correcting a class and setting out rules, but they are infused with a deep love for the people he is writing to, and a desire for the truth of Jesus to be continually heard. He writes with genuine enthusiasm, passion and wisdom that still applies to us today.

Find some of the books Paul wrote and just read the first few opening paragraphs of each letter. See for yourself how Paul had a genuine heart and interest as he shared incredible truths about Jesus to the churches.

23

24 Romans

'Everyone who calls on the name of the LORD will be saved.' **Romans 10:13**

Paul wanted to visit the Christians in Rome, who had possibly become Christians on the day of Pentecost and then established a church there. He wasn't able to get there, and so wrote this letter from Corinth (hence the books of 1 and 2 Corinthians, which come right after Romans), where he was staying.

The Christians in Rome were significant as Rome was the capital of the Roman Empire. The apostles hadn't yet been able to reach the Christians in Rome, so the church there needed instruction and teaching on what had been witnessed in Jerusalem during the life of Jesus. Paul wasn't writing to the believers in Rome to correct them, but to encourage and share truth and revelation with them about Jesus and what He had accomplished on the cross for all people.

Throughout this letter we read that God was at work, and lives were being set free by faith alone in Jesus Christ. And even though Jesus was the Messiah that God had promised to the Jewish people, He had died to save everyone. The gospel message wasn't just for Jews, but for anyone who would accept the love of Jesus. All of humanity was now invited to come and claim the free gift of life that Jesus had won for us all that day. And the news really was going viral!

Paul talks about three main themes within this letter: condemnation, justification and sanctification (some big words there, right?!). First, Paul shows that all of humanity needed a saviour. No one sits outside of the condemnation of sin and the penalty of death that was owed. Then, justification is the process of repair and restoring the possibility of a right relationship between humanity and God – Jesus bridged that gap, and because of Him, we can be in that restored relationship. Then Paul deals with sanctification, which is acquired through faith and is a process of being made holy. This is a new life made possible by the Holy Spirit as we accept Jesus and die to our old, sinful way of life.

The topics and themes in this letter can be a challenge to wrestle with. Take a look at some of these verses from Romans and spend some time reflecting on them during the day: Romans 1:16, 3:23, 5:1, 12:2.

25

Corinthians

'This means that anyone who belongs to Christ has become a new person. The old life is gone; a new life has begun!' **2 Corinthians 5:17**

The city of Corinth, in southern Greece, was a hive of activity that lots of trade and society passed through. Corinth was also a place for sports fans as it held the Isthmian games, which were not as big as the Olympics we have in modern times, but gathered a crowd for sure!

The trouble was, with so many cultural crossing points and being a centre for trade and commerce, Corinth became a place of very confused morals, values and identity. There were even 'priestesses' who were functioning as prostitutes in a twisted religious sex trade for locals and foreigners.

Paul had founded a church in Corinth and seen lives transformed by the truth of Jesus Christ. The problem was that the culture of the place was so strong that it continually caused issues for people in the church, who struggled to live out the Christian life when it looked so different to the lives of the people around them. This meant that division, trouble and conflict were rife in the church, and many people wanted to follow Jesus and His teaching but were being suffocated by the immorality in Corinth.

Paul speaks (or writes) directly into this situation, and his letters uncover stuff for the people there and realign their hearts and minds to the calling they had received to follow Jesus with all they have. Paul talks about unity, love and how to support and encourage one another in faith. He explores issues of marriage, roles for men and women, and church management and order. (It is important to consider that Paul was writing into specific issues of the time in Corinth.)

One of the great things about both these letters is that Paul continues to provide hope to the Church and remind it of the bigger picture. He does correct, challenge and urge action, but he also affirms and inspires hope and renewed vision, which the people in Corinth really needed to hear.

If you've ever been to a Christian wedding in the UK, you've probably heard 1 Corinthians 13:4-13 being read. Have another look at it today. How does it challenge modern ideas about what love is?

26

Galatians

'So Christ has truly set us free. Now make sure that you stay free, and don't get tied up again in slavery to the law.' **Galatians 5:1**

The world looked a bit different when the Bible was written. Asia Minor, as it was called, is where we can find modern-day Turkey, and that was where the Galatian churches were (who Paul was writing to in this letter). Paul travelled around Galatia and founded churches in the southern areas there, in places called Antioch, Iconium, Lystra and Derbe.

Paul writes to the churches in this area to encourage and inspire them, but also to try to head off false teaching that was going around and trying to pull people away from Christianity. The focus of this false teaching was to try to remove the idea that salvation is by faith in Jesus Christ alone.

Certain subversive groups and individuals argued that for Gentiles (non-Jewish people) to be saved, they must follow Jewish customs – in particular all the laws of Moses, including circumcision. But this was just a manipulation of the laws God gave Moses, and an attempt to hold people back under a load of rules they couldn't keep.

In light of this, Paul writes to these churches, urging them to hold the line and not allow these lies to deceive them or divert them from the truth. Salvation, argues Paul, is a gift that is accessed through faith in Jesus Christ, not something to be earned or achieved by the assimilation of Jewish customs and traditions.

During this time, Paul had lots of opposition, and many religious leaders and sects tried to undermine Paul's authority and witness. The message of the cross and of Jesus challenged the control and rule-based ritualism of the day that had blinded so many ultra-religious people to the simplicity of the cross. But Paul's letter to the Galatians brings them – and us – back to basics. Jesus is the real deal; it's about relationship, not religion.

Let's not complicate the simple message of the cross with tradition and customs. Have you seen and heard that simple message, a voice of hope and peace, purpose and forgiveness?

27

Ephesians

'Now all glory to God, who is able, through his mighty power at work within us, to accomplish infinitely more than we might ask or think.'

Ephesians 3:20

When Paul wrote this letter, Ephesus was in Asia Minor (now Turkey). Paul had been through a shipwreck and was in prison in Rome when he wrote this one, and it's amazing to think that in his own difficult situation he was able to encourage others like this.

Paul had a couple of friends called Priscilla and Aquila, who had helped him establish the Christian community in Corinth. He had stayed with them because they did a similar job; Paul didn't just share Jesus, he also worked as a tent-maker to help fund his travel, accommodation and food requirements. Priscilla and Aquila had travelled with Paul to Ephesus and they had been really helpful there, setting up the church that Paul later helped on one of his missionary visits.

This letter to the Christian church in Ephesus is from the heart. In the first three chapters, Paul recaps exactly what it is that Jesus won for us on the cross, and what our new identity is as a result of that win! In the rest of the letter, he explores what it looks like to live out the Christian life. Paul massively encourages the community and inspires them with big-picture thinking: they are not to follow Paul, but the God who can do all things. Paul repeatedly puts the focus back onto Jesus – he has no delusions of grandeur when it comes to himself.

Perhaps one of the best-known sections in this letter is Paul's instruction to the church to be equipped with the full 'armour of God'. It's a metaphor that we can all get on board with – kitting ourselves out from head to toe in God's love, peace, truth and righteousness. And Paul doesn't write about this 'armour' with a merely defensive stance – we march into battle, ready to fight. It's a victorious read – you'll be encouraged!

Take a look at the armour of God in Ephesians 6:10-18. What does each piece of armour represent to you?

28

Philippians

'And now, dear brothers and sisters, one final thing. Fix your thoughts on what is true, and honourable, and right, and pure, and lovely, and admirable. Think about things that are excellent and worthy of praise.'

Philippians 4:8

The next church was located in Philippi in Macedonia. Again, this is a letter that Paul wrote from prison.

Philippi was made part of the Roman Empire after a historic battle that took place there centuries before Paul's time. In Paul's era, Philippi was a place where lots of Roman army veterans lived in retirement. There was a strong sense of identity and pride in being Roman citizens in a colony like Philippi. Some Bible commentators suggest that you can see how Paul notes the culture around him in Philippians 3:20, when he describes followers of Christ as 'citizens of heaven'. In putting it like this, he's addressing his readers in language they'd understand.

However, it hadn't gone too well for Paul when he'd actually been in Philippi. In Acts 16:16-24 we read that on one occasion, Paul met a slave girl who was demon possessed and could speak about future events that, in turn, made her masters lots of money. After a time of being harassed by the girl, Paul rebuked the spirit (told it to leave the girl in Jesus' name), so the spirit left. Result! Only this meant the girl could no longer make money 'fortune telling' for her owners, who weren't too happy about it. They took Paul and his travelling companion, Silas, to the local authorities. The people kicked off and Paul and Silas found themselves taking a serious beating from the crowd, and then they got thrown into prison. However, the way they got out of that prison was amazing, and well worth checking out! You can find it in Acts 16:25-34.

Philippians is a great letter and it encouraged the church to hold on to Jesus and be living examples of the grace they had received. It's still a great encouragement to us today.

Have a think about your own sense of identity as a citizen - either of the whole nation or as a member of your local community. How does this compare with the idea of being a 'citizen of heaven'?

29

Colossians

'Devote yourselves to prayer with an alert mind and a thankful heart.'
Colossians 4:2

Colossae was a church Paul hadn't founded himself, but he loved them and he told them so. Just hearing about their faith encouraged him. Like many of the other letters Paul wrote, the letter to the Colossians focuses on dealing with some specific situations at the time, as well as encouraging and reaffirming some solid gospel teaching.

In this instance the church at Colossae had been confused and distracted by some false teaching. This teaching was very complex, and parts of it were later defined as something called 'Gnosticism'. You might be wondering if Gnosticism is something you need ointment for, but put into terms that I can just about grasp, Gnosticism is simply suggesting that, yes, God is good, but all matter is evil and bad. And some kind of special 'secret higher understanding' was needed to ever really find salvation. Of course, it was nonsense.

Paul was able to redirect and correct these false teachings and really show the church in Colossae the supremacy of Jesus Christ. The good news of Jesus is that He has done it all for us – we don't need any special, secret knowledge or to work our way up the ranks to a kind of 'higher order'. Because of Jesus, 'It is finished' – He has done it all.

Once again, Paul is a fan of bringing us back to basics. He drives home the message that we have new life in Christ – we cast off the old, dirty stuff, and 'put on' our new identity – one centered in love.

Have a little read of these verses from Colossians 1:21-23 and see what you think: 'This includes you who were once far away from God. You were his enemies, separated from him by your evil thoughts and actions. Yet now he has reconciled you to himself through the death of Christ in his physical body. As a result, he has brought you into his own presence, and you are holy and blameless as you stand before him without a single fault. But you must continue to believe this truth and stand firmly in it. Don't drift away from the assurance you received when you heard the Good News.'

---

30 The end

> 'Look! I stand at the door and knock. If you hear my voice and open the door, I will come in, and we will share a meal together as friends.' **Revelation 3:20**

We haven't been able to look at every book of the Bible, but hopefully by now you have had a rough outline of what's in it! Of course, this is only a brief overview of the big picture stuff, and when you really drill into the Bible for yourself you will be continually amazed and inspired by it, daily! But here we are at the end... in more ways than one.

Revelation is an 'uncovering', or a 'glimpse beneath the veil' of what is still to come, and it's pretty epic. The author of Revelation is John (one of the Gospel writers), who also wrote three letters in the New Testament (handily labelled as 1, 2 and 3 John).

John, the last survivor from among the apostles, gets a series of revelations from God when he is in old age. John had been living on the island of Patmos after having been banished there by the Romans for preaching Jesus.

The revelations John gets are prophetic, but also poetic in the way they are recorded. But above all, his visions are about Jesus' majesty and authority, showing Jesus as the glorified Son of God.

There are also revelations about seven churches that are called to account for different reasons. Then there are a series of revelations focused around eschatology, which means looking at how the world as we know it will end and a new one will begin.

If you want to explore Revelation in greater depth you will find that it is incredibly profound and has some striking poetic imagery. But don't be put off by that, because the book of Revelation does some simple things really well too.

John sees Jesus in glory as the Son of God, and is utterly overwhelmed by the experience. Jesus has been given all authority, all power and all majesty. The book of Revelation is a stark reminder that the end has not yet arrived, but it will. Jesus will return in glory and what a day that will be!

Have a look at Revelation 21:4-5.
How does this encourage you?

A note from Nathan

So, there we have it! You have reached the end of this whistle-stop tour, but more importantly, you have had a glimpse of the Bible and its relevance for your life. The Bible shows us more of God, who loves us so much that He gave His only Son to win us – you – back.

Win you back? Right from the very start, the Bible describes sin and how God has been continually calling people back to Him. Sin broke the relationship and heaven's answer was Jesus. This great mystery that builds up in the Bible is revealed to be one man: God's only Son, who had the most amazing life. He taught, spoke and lived like no other. He gave His life up on a cross, and three days later, God raised Him back to life. This is the message of grace, hope and love for us. We can be free men – free from the weight of sin, and the Bible calls that salvation.

This stuff is a choice. Your arms are not being forced up your back – you're not being pushed into a church. The choice is yours. You don't need to understand and memorise the Bible or be the perfect man – you just need to accept, ask Jesus into your life, and be forgiven. What a message!

Continue building your relationship with God

Lay the foundations of Christianity and build your relationship with God. Packed with 30 relevant Bible readings, practical points and prayers, these notes will help you navigate through your life and faith.

These Bible notes explore different themes to encourage and challenge. Written by Carl Beech and two guest contributors, each book contains two months of daily readings and prayers.

e Also available in eBook formats

Courses and seminars

Waverley Abbey College

Publishing and media

Conference facilities

Transforming lives

CWR's vision is to enable people to experience personal transformation through applying God's Word to their lives and relationships.

Our Bible-based training and resources help people around the world to:
- Grow in their walk with God
- Understand and apply Scripture to their lives
- Resource themselves and their church
- Develop pastoral care and counselling skills
- Train for leadership
- Strengthen relationships, marriage and family life and much more.

CWR Applying God's Word to everyday life and relationships

CWR, Waverley Abbey House,
Waverley Lane, Farnham,
Surrey GU9 8EP, UK

Telephone: **+44 (0)1252 784700**
Email: **info@cwr.org.uk**
Website: **www.cwr.org.uk**

Registered Charity No. 294387
Company Registration No. 1990308

Our insightful writers provide daily Bible reading notes and other resources for all ages, and our experienced course designers and presenters have gained an international reputation for excellence and effectiveness.

CWR's Training and Conference Centres in Surrey and East Sussex, England, provide excellent facilities in idyllic settings - ideal for both learning and spiritual refreshment.